Mountain Main

A Visual Journey into the Beauty of the Sawtooth's

Cary William White

Appreciation!

This book is quite simply a gift from our beloved Mother, Earth (and my new Nikon camera)! I was given life here (thank you Jack and Vera) to experience such loveliness. Thank you Joseph, for showing me, patiently and so very artistically, the way to walk in wilderness… and for those incredible gourmet camp dinners!

Mahalo!

Cary

Mountain Main by Cary William White
©Wildwood Pub 2012

First Printing, CreateSpace/Amazon.com, 2012

One – LaBois!

For the last five summers I have taken at least one, sometimes two excursions into the deep wild of the Sawtooth Wilderness Area, located South of Stanley, Idaho. In July of 2012, my hiking partner and I managed to have our most breath-taking, unforgettable journey of our lives. In this little book, which celebrates this auspicious and dangerous journey, I hope to share with you some of the wonder in which we partook. Enjoy!

We had just reached the summit at 9500 feet, overlooking two entire canyons on either side. Tohobit Peak sits above me like a hat.
If you care to count, there are at least five ranges viewed behind us...five vast canyons, five disparate sets of mountain peaks.

The journey begins with our home, Boise Idaho. Set beneath the foothills and Bogus Basin Mountains, with the Owyhee range 50 miles guarding our 'south-western' end, Boise or La Bois as the French speaking Indians called her, was at one time also known as the Valley of Peace... a haven of abundant wildlife, game, water and fertile fields where countless tribes would gather, in peace to enjoy the heavenly valley of plenty.

Two - The Wild

The Sawtooth Wilderness Area, part of the Rocky Mountain Range, was first designated as a Primitive Area, protected by the U.S. Government in 1937 consists of over 217,088 acres. There are 40 trails (350 miles worth), most of which were constructed in the 1960's. There are over 50 peaks over 10,000 feet high, with Thompson Peak being the tallest in the range and wilderness. (see below, courtesy of Wikipedia).

The trailhead for Fish Hook Creek Canyon (7200 feet), our destination, is accessed from the Redfish Lake trail parking lot. After we parked, loaded up our 40-plus pound packs, we began our ascent up the trail. The first three miles, mostly scrub brush, sage, and dirt with just a sprinkling of trees is our first day of hiking (first yellow ball). By the time we reach the middle lake of the right hand canyon we will have climbed seven miles up to reach 9500 feet.

View on the way up the canyon, second day of hiking. Though late in July, this is early spring for this the upper part of the Area. There were millions of flowers, grasses, brush and shrubbery…green, yellow, orange, violet, ultra blue, scarlet red… beautiful!

Three – In Our Midst, in Her Midst

The third day we had made it to a 8900 feet and one day's hike to the lake that was our destination (see GoogleEarth Map-1). We took a day of rest then began the steep hike another 300 feet up the hill.

Four – Goat Feet

As we climbed the trackless, rugged, rocky terrain up our mere 300 feet of altitude, the going was slow with the heavy packs, and the fatigued muscles. But we had the previous day of rest to prepare us for this climb, and we made it.

Walking through the wonder

    Green and Rock, everywhere

No words to speak, sights too vast to even conceive

    Climb, step, stumble, keep on… one more step higher, look how high you've come!

Love is good

Five - Moon-lit Ebert and Lake

Joseph had miss-calculated our trajectory. We crossed several creeks, thinking we were headed toward to lower, easier to climb to lake. We were wrong. Our steep ridge that had us taking breathers every 20 minutes, had lead us to the Middle Lake. One lake above our intended destination. But Eureka! What a view!

We arrived about three hours before dusk to this clear lake and Mountain View. Mount Ebert, gleaming the morning and evening sun, full moon lit lake, forest, rock and hills, all filled with trees, grasses, flowers and such brimming, tender, fragile, life.

Six – Fish in the Clouds

It took us five grueling days to hike the six miles of trail-less ground and slopes to reach our base camp at the lake, feeling the elation of having gone further than we had originally aimed. By the next morning we could still not quite get over just how beautiful this isolated lake setting was. And we had it to ourselves. We had only seen a handful of hikers the entire week so far, so the quiet and undisturbed beauty was truly exceptional.

Knowing it would take two days to return to Redfish and the car, leaving us two whole days to have day hikes into the surrounding canyons and lakes. Our first day hike we chose to ascend to the basin that fed our lake. Once there we could see the shape of a fish in the middle lake, just below the basin tarn containing the fresh snow-melt from the basin glacier. It was the purest, clearest light blue lake we had ever seen.

Seven - Summit!

During our hike the sixth day, as we reached the fish shaped lake and its tarn basin, we both looked up at the canyon wall and wondered if we could climb to the summit to see the spectacle of two entire canyons, sets of peaks and adjoining lakes. We wondered, pondered and finally decided that the climb would be too much, too difficult, and very precariously dangerous. So we headed back to camp.

Our seventh day we had determined to climb the canyon heading past the Steven's lake canyon, proceeding up to the high basin directly above us to the right. It was a fairly long hike, full of wonders, lakes, rivulets, and tarns.

Our first treat was this little lake, which was our original destination, and though immense in beauty, color and fauna, was not quite the haven of our Ebert Moon Lake. We took some extra time to enjoy the songs eminating from the creek feeding the lake. It even inspired us to sing a line or two of Amazing Grace.

After leaving the inlet and the lake, we began the ascent to the foremost basin. There were lots of rocks and boulders that has chipped off and stumbled down the steep mountain slopes. One rock had broken into two large slabs, ingeniously folded together, a makeshift cave. It looked like a great place to take a break from the intense sun and eat some lunch.

As we crawled under the ledge of one of the slanted rocks forming half of the roof of this ominous cavern, we paused and listed in silence. First one, then two, eventually five different tones of moving water could be discerned. There were massive amounts of water being filtered through underground crags, channels and causeways right beneath our feet, visible only to our ears and the vibration of the rock supporting our feet.

One of the tones was almost imperceptible: the tone of deep underground water produced a pitch human ears can barely detect. The hum of this earthy baritone bass filled us with awe and inspiration to mimic. If only one could sing that low!

After our brief lunch, free concert of the water and rocks, and break from the intense high mountain sun, we resumed our hike up the canyon's debris-filled slope.

Then quite suddenly, to both our great surprise and delight, we beheld the summit pass. Joseph had mentioned we might find a way to the top, after all, the evening before. But now, here we were viewing a pass that was passable! We ventured forth, to The Summit!

Once we climbed to the apex between two disparate world views, literally, we stood in glee as we beheld the Sawtooth Lake valley and peaks on one side, then to our backs was the canyon we just emerged from, containing all the lakes, canyons and peaks we had explored the six days before. The White Cloud Range loomed in the distance below us, some fifty miles away.

The Halstead fire looms and smolders in the distance. Sawtooth Lake, offset in its own quiet beauty.

From this summit view we could view five distinct mountain ranges, layer upon layer, miles of canyon, creeks, lakes, and trees filling each gap between.

Eight - Recollection

By the time we reached our home at the lake, we were pleasantly exhausted and elated. The previous days ascent had made us strong, providing momentous victories and delights with each passing day. Having finally reached a summit, as well as having the best view in the universe...full moon, quite lake interrupted gently by the feeding trout, tender yet resilient plant life and trees, myriad of rock, crag, slope and peak engulfing, cradling these two pioneers.

Nine – Homebound

It was day eight, evening's end, knowing we would be hiking down the last half way to Redfish Lake the next day, but the last thing we wanted was to ever leave this place. This heaven. Things seem so perfectly balanced up here. There's no drama, no 'problema's', no stress, like there is in the city.

The only thing one can do when faced with this kind of challenge (going back to hell when heaven suites you better...) is too take the Mountain with you. Keep it ever-fresh, ever-green in the mind, the soul, the heart. After all, this life here is really just a reflection of what each living being really is...all the immense glory of nature rolled into a silly two-legged creature built to explore, roam, and be witness to the outer reflection of Self.

Final word? Sure.....

Salute'

Publications by Cary William White:

The Complete Guitar Self Learning Program (Amazon)

Smiling Rivers Anthology- 30 years of Song Crafting (CD Amazon)

Melodious One – Collection of original and classical instrumentals (Amazon)

Portal Through the Sun- Fantasy/Science Fiction (Amazon.com)

Mountain Main - Coffee-table Photography/Storybook – (Amazon)

The Energy Dynamics of Learning (Amazon)

www.ingramcontent.com/pod-product-compliance
Lightning Source LLC
Chambersburg PA
CBHW060824290526
45792CB00005BB/1790